Woods, Geraldine

Animal experimentation and testing:
a pro/con issue

Animal Experimentation and Testing

A Pro/Con Issue

Geraldine Woods

Enslow Publishers, Inc.

40 Industrial Road	PO Box 38
Box 398	Aldershot
Berkeley Heights, NJ 07922	Hants GU12 6BP
USA	UK

http://www.enslow.com

Library of Congress Cataloging-in-Publication Data

Woods, Geraldine.
    Animal experimentation and testing : a pro/con issue / Geraldine Woods.
        p. cm. — (Hot pro/con issues)
    Includes bibliographical references and index.
    Summary: Examines both sides of the debate on animal experimentation and testing, as well as possible alternatives to such experimentation.
    ISBN 0-7660-1191-7
    1. Animal experimentation—Juvenile literature. 2. Vivisection—Juvenile literature. [1. Animal experimentation. 2. Vivisection. 3. Animals—Treatment.] I. Title. II. Series.
HV4915. W66   1999
179'.4—dc21   98-49076
                                                            CIP
                                                            AC

Printed in the United States of America

10 9 8 7 6 5 4 3 2 1

To Our Readers:
All Internet addresses in this book were active and appropriate when we went to press. Any comments or suggestions can be sent by e-mail to Comments@enslow.com or to the address on the back cover.

Illustration Credits: AP/Wide World Photos, pp. 5, 17, 45, 50, 54; © Corel Corporation, pp. 1, 4, 9; People for the Ethical Treatment of Animals, pp. 21, 33.

Cover Illustration: People for the Ethical Treatment of Animals

Contents

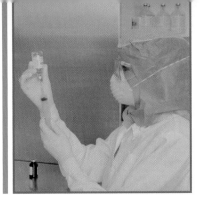

If you are reading this book, you probably like animals. Dr. Jonathan Balcombe of The Humane Society of the United States has a message for you. "You've probably seen that animals enjoy life," says Dr. Balcombe. "A cat will purr. A dog will wag its tail and roll over. If they feel pain, they yelp and run away. It is not nice to put them in small cages, to cut them open, to inject them with things that will harm them."[1]

If you are reading this book, you probably also have an interest in science. Dr. John Miller, the head of an association that inspects and accredits laboratories, has a message for you too. He wants you to think of people who are suffering from serious diseases. "Visit a children's hospital," he says, "a cancer center. If you had to kill ten rats to help those children, wouldn't you? Researchers do what they do because it is going to help human beings."[2]

These two scientists are on opposite sides of a very important question: Is it right to use animals in research? Can the other creatures that share our planet be placed in a laboratory? Do medical and scientific discoveries justify the suffering of the animals? And if animal experiments are ended, will humans suffer instead?

From 18 to 22 million animals a year are used in American research laboratories.[3] No one knows the exact number because rats, mice, fish, and birds

*T*wo rhesus monkeys, part of a cloning experiment, huddle together at the Oregon Regional Primate Research Center.

are not reported to the Department of Agriculture, the government agency that gathers statistics. In the last twenty years, the trend is to use fewer animals. According to the Department of Agriculture, about 2.2 million animals were used in laboratories.[4] In 1997 the number was about one million less. (Neither number includes rats, mice, fish, or birds.)[5]

The numbers have been dropping partly because of pressure from the animal rights movement. Animal rights activists believe that animals have the right to a life that is natural and free from harm by human beings. They believe that it is wrong to conduct experiments on animals unless the animal itself will benefit from the study.

Disagreeing with this view are supporters of biomedical research, or experimentation on living animals. (Biomedical research is sometimes called "vivisection." In recent years some scientists have objected to the word *vivisection*.) Those who support biomedical research believe that helping human beings is the most important task. They say that animals may be used as necessary to make people's lives better.

In this book, you will read how animals are used in research and how people's attitudes toward them have changed throughout history. You will also read about nonanimal methods of research. Finally, you will hear arguments for and against the use of animals in laboratories. Listen, think, and then decide for yourself where you stand on this important issue.

Chapter 1

A Historical View of Animals in Research

The belief that human beings are more important than other creatures is very old. In the Old Testament of the Bible, God gives humanity power over "the fish of the sea and over the birds of the air . . . and over all the earth and over every creeping thing that creeps upon the earth."[1] Aristotle (384–322 B.C.), an ancient Greek philosopher, believed that only humans can think. Therefore, Aristotle said, we have the right to use animals as we wish.[2] Thomas Aquinas (A.D. 1225–1274), an important Christian thinker, wrote that animals lack souls and therefore have no rights.[3] Other religions teach that animals do have souls.

Rene Descartes (A.D. 1596–1650), a French philosopher and scientist, lived at a time when magic and theory were being replaced by observation and experiment. Descartes believed that only humans could think and feel. He saw animals as machines and compared the cries of a laboratory animal to the squeak of a clock spring. Descartes said people have the right to use animals just as if they were machines.[4]

Most people who experimented with animals in the seventeenth century probably did not agree with Descartes. After all, they could see a dog yelp in pain or a cat cry. However, in Descartes's time most scientists thought that their experiments were more important than the animals' feelings.[5]

Animals in Research and Medicine

Animals have been used in research for more than two thousand years. Alcmaeon of Croton (born about 500 B.C.) was a Greek doctor. Alcmaeon experimented on living animals, cutting a nerve behind the eye in order to study vision. Erasistratus (born about 300 B.C.) was a professor at a medical school in Alexandria, Egypt. Erasistratus tried to understand the workings of the human heart and brain by studying the hearts and brains of animals.[6] Pliny the Elder (born about A.D. 24) was an ancient Roman scholar. He studied the structure of the body, probably by operating on live animals.[7] Galen (A.D. 130–200), a Greek doctor, also experimented on animals. His work with apes and pigs led to the discovery that veins carried blood.[8] Early Chinese scientists made medications from pigs, deer, sheep, and other animals. In seventh-century China, for example, a doctor named Chen Ch'uan wrote about pills made from the dried thyroid glands of one hundred sheep.[9] In the ninth century an Arab scientist named Ibn Mussawaih dissected monkeys to study the structure of the animals' bodies.[10] (To dissect is to cut into a dead body, carefully separating the organs for study.)

By the seventeenth century, doctors in Italy were dissecting animals to examine the way their stomachs and nerves work. In 1628, the English doctor William Harvey described how blood circulates in the human body. To accomplish this task, Harvey experimented with living animals and dissected human corpses.[11]

In the nineteenth century Louis Pasteur, a French scientist, grew deadly germs for a disease called anthrax. He made a vaccine from weakened germs. (Vaccines protect the body against specific diseases.) Pasteur injected the anthrax vaccine into healthy animals. He exposed the injected animals and another group of untreated animals to the disease. The vaccinated animals remained healthy. The cows, sheep, and goats that had not received the vaccine died.

*O*ne experiment in seventh-century China used the dried thyroid glands of one hundred sheep.

During the nineteenth and twentieth centuries many vaccines were developed. The vaccines were often tested first on live animals and later on a small number of people. Diseases like polio, diphtheria, tetanus, and rabies had once killed millions of people. Now they were reduced or even wiped out by the new vaccines.

In the twentieth century many new medicines and techniques like open-heart surgery, organ transplants, and radiation treatment have been developed through animal experimentation.[12]

Animals in Psychological Research

Some scientists working with animals have studied the mind, not the body. One famous experiment by Ivan Pavlov (1849–1936), a Russian researcher, involved dogs. Pavlov rang a bell many times when food was given to dogs. Then he rang a bell and provided no food. The dogs acted as if a meal were about to appear. Pavlov said that the dogs were "conditioned" to associate hunger with the sound of the bell.[13]

Other Uses

In recent years animals have been used to test household cleaners, makeup, shampoo, and other substances. Manufacturers want to know whether the chemicals in their products cause skin or eye problems or are harmful to humans. The Food and Drug Administration (FDA), an agency of the United States government, requires companies to show that their products are not likely to harm the people who use them properly. Products that have not undergone a long series of tests must carry warning labels stating that the products may be dangerous. The FDA requires animal tests for medicines and eye-care products. Companies that make cosmetics and personal products like soap and toothpaste do not have to test their products on animals. However, many do.[14]

Many products now carry labels stating that the products are "cruelty free" or "not tested on animals." Some of the products labeled this way were tested only by nonanimal experiments. But sometimes these labels are misleading. Separate ingredients in the product might have been tested on animals in the past. Or the manufacturer might buy animal test results from another company.[15]

School is another place to find laboratory animals. Since the 1920s the dead bodies of animals such as frogs, worms, grasshoppers, unborn pigs, cats, and other animals have been used to teach the structure of the animal's body. A high school biology class, for example, might dissect a frog. Older students might work on animals with more complicated body structures, like an unborn pig, a rabbit, or a cat.

The use of animals in medicine, psychology, and education has surely increased the understanding of our bodies and the world. Yet all this work has been accompanied by questions. Did the animals suffer? Was there any other way to obtain the same knowledge? And most recently, do human beings have the right to experiment on animals at all?

Chapter 2

Animal Welfare and Animal Rights

The question is not can they reason? nor, can they talk? but can they suffer?"[1] That's what Jeremy Bentham (1748–1832), an English philosopher, said about Descartes's view of animals as "tools." Bentham thought that Descartes asked the wrong questions about animals. Bentham knew that animals feel pain. Therefore, he said, they should not suffer and die at the hands of human beings.

Bentham was not the only one to object to the use of animals in laboratories. Samuel Johnson (1709–1784), a British scholar, did not believe that animal experiments produced any useful information. Even if the experiments helped human beings, Johnson said, such research was still wrong. To cause innocent creatures pain, in Johnson's view, was never right.[2]

Many experiments caused pain. Until the late 1840s, researchers used no anesthetics (drugs that numb the body or bring on sleep). So animals that had been infected with a disease or that had been operated on suffered greatly.

In 1831 a British scientist named Marshall Hall applied the ideas of animal welfare to science. He listed rules that should govern the use of animals in laboratories:

> ➤ An experiment should never be performed on an animal if simple observation will give enough information.

> ➤ All experiments should have a clear, reachable goal.

> ➤ Scientists should check the work of other researchers to be sure that they are not repeating an experiment.

> ➤ Animals should suffer as little as possible. Animals that have less ability to think should be used whenever possible. [In other words, it is better to experiment with a worm than with a chimpanzee.][3]

The Antivivisection Movement

Hall's rules were criticized by antivivisectionists. They believe that vivisection is always cruel. One antivivisectionist was Frances Power Cobbe (1822–1904), a British woman who founded the first society dedicated to ending animal research completely. Cobbe's group was called the Society for the Protection of Animals Liable to Vivisection. ["Liable to Vivisection" means "likely to be used in an experiment."] In the United States, Henry Bergh also worked for the welfare of animals. Bergh founded the American Society for the Prevention of Cruelty to Animals (ASPCA) in 1866. The ASPCA was modeled after a British group, the Royal Society for the Prevention of Cruelty to Animals (RSPCA). The RSPCA was established in 1824. Both

Important Dates in the American Animal Rights Movement

1866—Henry Bergh founds the American Society for the Prevention of Cruelty to Animals (ASPCA).

1873—American Anti-Vivisection Society established.

1892—The American Humane Association calls for an end to painful experiments intended to teach or demonstrate well-known facts.

1951—Christine Stevens founds the Animal Welfare Institute.

1954—The Humane Society of the United States is established.

1959—The "three R's of animal experimentation"—replace, reduce, refine—are stated.

1966—The Animal Welfare Act is passed.

1970—The Animal Welfare Act now covers more animals and requires pain relief.

1971—The Animal Welfare Act now specifically states that rats, mice, and birds are not covered.

1975—Peter Singer publishes *Animal Liberation*, arguing the philosophy of animal rights.

1980—Ingrid Newkirk and Alex Pacheco form People for the Ethical Treatment of Animals (PETA).

1981—Center for Alternatives to Animal Testing is established.

1985—The Animal Welfare Act now requires exercise for dogs and attention to the mental health of monkeys and apes.

1987—Band of Mercy, an animal rights group, steals pigs and cats from the Department of Agriculture Animal Parisitology Institute lab; Jenifer Graham, a high school student who opposes dissection, sues for the right to refuse the assignment. She is graded on an alternative lesson.

1989—The Animal Liberation Front (ALF) burglarizes lab at Texas Tech University Health Science Center; research on sudden infant death syndrome lost, five cats stolen.

1990—Animal activists sue to have rats, mice, and birds, included in the Animal Welfare Act. They win the case but later lose on appeal.

1992—ALF firebombs five trucks carrying meat; ALF break-in at Michigan State University—research on pollution and wildlife diseases lost, as well as research on in vitro testing.

1998—American Anti-Vivisection Society petitions Department of Agriculture to include rats, mice, and birds in the Animal Welfare Act.

societies are still in existence today, and both oppose vivisection. They work for the welfare of all animals. Around the turn of the century many other organizations—the American Anti-Vivisection Society, for example—were established specifically to fight the use of animals in scientific research experiments.[4]

Although the antivivisectionists worked tirelessly, they had little success in the early twentieth century. Medical science made a number of important discoveries in that period, and public support for research grew.[5]

➤ The Modern Animal Rights Movement

In 1975 a book entitled *Animal Liberation* was published. Author Peter Singer says that yes, animals cannot talk or reason in the same way as human beings. Singer points out that animals, however, think and feel in their own way. Because of this fact, animals deserve the same consideration as human beings. Singer's ideas belong to a philosophy called utilitarianism. In utilitarianism, the welfare of human beings must be weighed against the bad effects an experiment has on animals. Singer used a new word in his book: *speciesist*. Just as a racist believes that one race is better than another or a sexist believes that one sex is better than the other, a speciesist favors one species—humans—over animals. Singer says that speciesists are wrong. Humans are animals, too, and we must respect other species.[6]

Tom Regan took Singer's ideas a step further in his book *The Case for Animal Rights*, published in 1983. Regan believes that animals, like people, have rights. According to Regan, animals should not be in experiments at all. Even if great good would result, animals should not be treated as if they are the tools of human beings.[7]

The animal rights movement gained a great deal of support in 1981. In that year Alex Pacheco volunteered to work at the Institute for Behavioral Research in Silver Springs, Maryland. But Pacheco was not just a lab volunteer. He was an undercover investigator. Pacheco was horrified by what he saw in researcher Edward Taub's lab. Monkeys had nerves cut in one or both arms. Dr. Taub put the animals in situations where they needed to use the damaged body part. He wanted to see how the monkeys' bodies tried to overcome the damage. The doctor thought that someday his findings might help people with nerve damage. However, in the meantime, the monkeys were in terrible shape. Some had dislocated bones. One monkey had chewed off parts of every finger on one hand.[8]

Pacheco soon joined with Ingrid Newkirk, the founder of a new group called People for the Ethical Treatment of Animals (PETA). PETA is an animal rights organization. The group's motto is "Animals are not ours to eat, wear, experiment on, or use in entertainment.[9]

Pacheco took a camera to work with him. He secretly took pictures of the animals and the conditions under which they lived. Then he sent the film to the media. After the pictures became public, Edward Taub was charged with cruelty to animals. Dr. Taub was eventually found not guilty, although he was told to correct some violations in his laboratory.

The Silver Spring monkey incident brought much public attention to the issue of animals in laboratories. In 1980, fewer than twenty people belonged to PETA. By the early 1990s, PETA had more than four hundred thousand members.[10] In the 1980s, many other groups formed to work for animal welfare or animal rights. Today PETA, like many of these other groups, works to educate the public through a newsletter and pamphlets. It organizes protests against what it sees as unfair treatment of animals, and it sends undercover investigators into laboratories. PETA also publishes a list of companies that do not perform animal testing. PETA organizes boycotts (refusal to buy products) against companies that test on animals.

In recent years, a small number of radical animal rights groups have become violent. The Federal Bureau of Investigation has named the Animal Liberation Front (ALF) as a terrorist group. In 1991 members of ALF stole animals from a laboratory in Cook County Hospital in Chicago.[11] ALF and other extremist groups have also destroyed papers and experiments and even firebombed buildings.

Most animal activists do not approve of ALF's actions. However, they are also determined to end, by peaceful means, the use of animals in laboratories.

In 1998, two brands of panettone, a dessert bread, had to be withdrawn from stores in Italy. The ALF said they had poisoned the products because they allegedly included genetically engineered ingredients.

Chapter 3

How Animals Are Used in Research and Testing

One day in 1950, Italian scientist Rita Levi-Montalcini killed several mice. The mice had cancer, a serious disease in which the body's cells grow uncontrollably and form a mass called a tumor. Dr. Levi-Montalcini attached small bits of tumor to the bodies of unborn chickens. She found that some substance in the cancer cells caused extra nerves to grow in the developing chicken. Dr. Levi-Montalcini named this substance Nerve Growth Factor (NGF). The doctor won a Nobel Prize for her discovery of NGF. Someday her work may help fight ailments like multiple sclerosis or paralysis, conditions in which nerves are damaged.[1]

Dr. Levi-Montalcini's research is only one way animals are used in laboratories. Researchers also try new treatments on animals before testing them in human patients. Sometimes they purposely infect animals with a disease to study its symptoms and to test possible cures. For example, chimpanzees and other animals have been given injections of HIV, the virus that causes acquired immune deficiency syndrome (AIDS). In chimpanzees, the virus is called SIV. People with AIDS become very ill, but chimpanzees show few effects. However, researchers who use them to study AIDS believe that valuable information can still be learned from these experiments.[2]

Scientists have also bred animals so that they have a tendency to develop a specific disease, like leukemia (a cancer). After testing drugs or medical procedures on these animals, doctors move to human subjects.[3]

Genetic Engineering

When Cynthia Cutshall was born, doctors thought she would have a very short life. Cynthia had a condition called ADA Deficiency. Her body lacked the ability to fight infection. Following a procedure they had tested in animals, scientists took white blood cells from Cynthia and examined the genes. White blood cells are the infection fighters of the body.

Genes are like blueprints the body uses to create new cells. A faulty gene causes ADA Deficiency. Doctors took the bad genes out of Cynthia's cells and replaced them with new ones they had taken from healthy people. The new genes would enable Cynthia's body to manufacture her own infection fighters. They injected the changed cells into Cynthia, and she recovered.

The work that scientists did with Cynthia's blood cells is called "genetic engineering." This important scientific technique requires animals for research. Techniques for identifying, changing, and replacing genes were developed after experiments with millions of animals.[4] Mostly rats and mice are used because these animals grow to adulthood very quickly. Researchers can study several generations in a short time.[5] Also, the genetic code of a mouse or a rat seems to react like that of a human being in many cases.

Researchers perform genetic studies in several ways. To identify a gene, scientists might remove it from a mouse and see how the animal develops without it. Or they might study the genes of many animals with a specific disease (breast cancer, for example). If they find the same faulty gene in all the animals, they know that it plays a role in the disease. Then they look for a similar gene in human cells. Using these techniques, doctors have identified almost five thousand inherited disorders in humans.

Scientists also place the genes of one species into another. For example, some human genes have been inserted into pigs. The pigs then manufacture human insulin, an important body chemical. It is harvested and made into a medicine for people with diabetes, who cannot make their own insulin.[6]

The Draize Eye Test

Are your eyelashes too pale? Women who answered yes to this question in 1920 might have visited a beauty salon for a treatment with a dye named Lash Lure. However, along with a new image many customers received something extra: irritated eyes, blindness, and even, in one case, death.

A number of tests, some involving animals, have been developed to prevent the kind of injuries caused by Lash Lure. One is the Draize eye test, which checks whether a substance will harm the eyes. White rabbits are often used because their eyes do not easily wash away irritating substances. The rabbits are placed in boxes or held by metal bands so that they cannot move their heads. Then, the chemical being tested is dripped into their eyes. The rabbits' eyes are checked regularly to see if they are damaged.[7]

LD50 Test

The LD50 test was created in 1927 by a British scientist. "LD" stands for "lethal (fatal) dose." The "50" represents 50 percent. In the LD50 test, the test chemical is given to a group of animals in stronger and stronger doses. When half of the animals die, the lethal dose for 50 percent of the animals (the LD50) has been reached. For an adult human, salt has an LD50 of 1 quart, and nicotine (found in cigarettes) has an LD50 of half a teaspoon.[8]

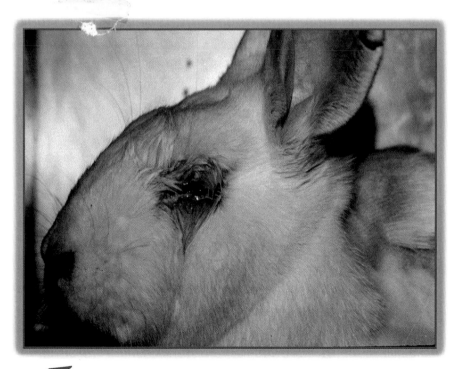

*T*his rabbit's eye is injured from an eye irritancy test for a men's cologne.

Other Tests

In the Draize skin test, a small shaved area of skin is covered with the chemical being tested. As in the eye test, the skin is examined for redness, swelling, and other signs of irritation. Draize skin tests are performed on rats, mice, rabbits, or other animals. To test the effect of a substance on breathing, animals might be placed in a closed container or forced to breathe through a mask. The substance to be tested is pumped into the mask. Hair spray, deodorants, spray cleaners, and other products are studied this way. To see whether a product causes cancer, mice and other animals are fed large quantities of a substance and then watched to see whether they develop a disease. This test is sometimes done with pregnant animals to see if the babies are born with any damage.[9]

Practice for Doctors

Animals are also used to teach health workers how to care for wounds, set bones, or treat other ailments. The United States Department of Defense has operated "wound labs" since 1957. In the wound laboratories, animals have been shot with weapons that soldiers are likely to face on the battlefield. Military doctors learn what type of wounds may result and how to treat them by practicing on the animals. The military has also exposed animals to fire and radiation to see what the effects might be on human troops. In nonmilitary medical training, doctors or medical students sometimes learn to perform surgery on dogs or pigs. Cats, dogs, ferrets, and pigs may be used for practice in inserting tubes into the stomach or breathing passages.

Not surprisingly, some people who work for animal welfare and animal rights have criticized all of these tests, particularly the Draize tests and the LD50. Henry Spira, a New York City teacher and a believer in animal rights, was one of the first to take the battle to the public. On April 15, 1980, he placed a full-page advertisement in *The New York Times* asking, "How many rabbits has Revlon [a cosmetics company] blinded for beauty's sake?" Revlon soon donated $750,000 for research into nonanimal tests. Because of pressure from animal activists, many companies now use alternatives to the Draize and LD50 tests. When these tests are done today, they generally use fewer animals and testing methods that cause less pain.[10]

Chapter 4

Testing Without Animals

The lab table holds shallow glass dishes, each with a small dab of what looks like jelly. The "jelly" is really a culture—a food that keeps cells alive. Some human skin cells are placed in each dish. Chemicals that are being tested—ingredients of shampoos, household cleaners, and so forth—are added. Then a dye is mixed in. Living cells take in the dye, but dead cells do not. Soon the color of the dishes shows how many cells are alive. In some dishes the jelly is clear (all cells are dead). In others it is pink (some cells are dead) or red (most cells are alive). Researchers analyze the color with a computer. The computer can calculate how likely a chemical is to kill human cells.[1]

This test, the Neutral Red Uptake Assay, is an "in vitro" experiment. In vitro experiments are performed without the use of animals. In vitro means "in glass." The name probably comes from the glass test tubes common in laboratories. Animal tests are sometimes called "in vivo" or "in life" tests. Scientists have always performed some in vitro tests. More are being developed every year.

Cell Cultures

In 1952, a woman dying of cancer allowed some of the cancer cells to be taken from her body. Her cancer cells started a colony of cells that provides the basis for some current experiments.[2] Cells from other parts of the human body have also been grown in cultures and then used in experiments. For example, cells from lungs test the effects of smoke and gases. Cancerous cells can also be grown in human muscle tissue that was removed during surgery. These cells form the basis of many experiments. Scientists have also succeeded in keeping heart cells alive and beating for almost three months. The cells have been used to test new heart drugs.[3]

Researchers have created artificial organs from human cells and other ingredients. TESTSKIN and NeoDerm are artificial skins. TESTLUNG is an artificial lung. These organs are used in wound and drug research.

Animal cells are also employed for in vitro work. Instead of hundreds of animals for one experiment, a single pig liver might supply a hundred experiments. Microscopic creatures like bacteria and yeast are also used in experiments. In the Ames test, bacteria are exposed to chemicals. If the bacteria's genes show damage, the chemical is suspected of causing cancer in humans.[4]

Other tests rely on plants. EYETEX examines the effect of adding a chemical to a protein extracted from beans. The way the protein reacts helps predict whether the chemical will irritate human eyes. SKINTEX uses a substance made from pumpkins to see if a chemical will harm human skin.[5]

Chemical and Computer Studies

By analyzing exactly how one chemical or drug harms the body, researchers try to predict whether a similar chemical will also be dangerous. A computer program checks the structure of a new drug to see whether it will interact with P450, a substance in the human body. If the new drug "locks" onto P450, it will probably be dangerous.

In another type of test, the chemical is put into a machine called a pH meter. The pH number tells whether the chemical is a neutral (like water), an acid (like lemon juice), or a base (like baking soda). Very strong acids or bases always irritate human skin and eyes, so they are rejected without further testing.[6]

Epidemiology: Medical Surveys

Information on medical history, eating, exercise, and other habits is often collected through surveys of large groups of people or from medical records. The study of this kind of information is called epidemiology. By analyzing the data, scientists try to determine what behavior puts people at risk. For example, in 1948 doctors began to investigate the habits of the residents of Framingham, a small town in Massachusetts. The doctors wanted to understand the causes of heart disease. For decades the people of Framingham have answered questions about their diet and lifestyle. They receive regular physical examinations. Researchers found that people who smoke, do not exercise, or have high blood pressure run a greater risk of heart disease. In 1951 similar studies in Britain showed a link between smoking and lung cancer.[7] Recently, scientists have analyzed many cases of sudden infant death syndrome (SIDS). With SIDS, a healthy infant suddenly dies for an unexplained reason. Researchers have found that certain sleeping positions and overheated rooms may increase the risk of SIDS.[8] Right now surveys are helping scientists investigate foods that seem to help the body resist cancer.

Human "Experiments"

Doctors often observe people who are ill to learn about the causes or progress of various diseases. People who have suffered brain damage from a stroke or a tumor, for example, might be given a word test. Doctors compare the parts of the brain that have been damaged to the patients' ability to use language. Then they map the speech centers of the brain. CAT scans and MRIs are machines that use magnetism, computers, and other factors to provide images of the inside of the body. These machines give much more information than X rays.

People sometimes volunteer to be the subjects of psychology experiments or to be the final testers of drugs and treatments that have been proved reasonably safe. People also test pesticides (substances that kill insects or plant pests).[9] However, scientists must be sure to explain all the possible risks before any testing begins and to obtain the person's consent. Some human beings contribute to science even after they are dead by allowing an autopsy (cutting into the body to observe and analyze its parts).

Education

Instead of working with animals, some medical schools provide in vitro practice. For example, students may operate on a human placenta. The placenta is an organ that provides nourishment to a baby before birth. The mother's body discards the placenta naturally.[10] Some medical schools provide special life-size dolls or human corpses that have been donated to science. Students use them to practice inserting breathing or food tubes. Also, many surgical students train by assisting experienced surgeons in actual operations or by working with lifelike computer programs. High school and college students may also work with computer programs and models instead of dead animals.

The Three R's

In vitro tests help scientists follow the first of the "three R's." The three R's were written in the 1950s by two scientists, William Russell and Rex Burch. The three R's are replacement, reduction, and refinement.[11] The first R *replaces* animals with alternatives, like the in vitro tests described above. The next R is *reduce*. Many traditional animal tests, like the Draize, are now used much less frequently than they were years ago. Not every industry uses the Draize tests in the same way, but some companies have also greatly reduced the number of rabbits in each test. The cosmetic industry, for example, performed Draize tests on 87 percent fewer animals between 1980 and 1989.[12] The last R is *refine*. The experiment is designed so that it causes less pain or distress. Refinement might be changing the way an animal is dosed (with a medicine) or changing the way an animal is killed at the end of an experiment. In some Draize tests, the rabbits receive an anesthetic in their eyes before the test. If irritation occurs, the eye may be washed immediately. Previously, no anesthetic was applied and the chemical was left in for days. Another type of refinement is to substitute an animal that seems to be less aware.

Some current experiments are conducted only in vitro, but many combine both animal and in vitro testing. This combination is called tier testing. In tier testing, an experiment follows a specific order. First, in vitro tests rule out chemicals that are certain to be dangerous. Then, a small number of animals might be used. Finally, tests are done on human volunteers. In another form of tier testing, drugs or treatments that look promising in computer models or in cell culture tests are later tried on animals.[13]

Chapter 5

Animal Experimentation and the Law

On a sunny afternoon in October 1997, seven people sat around a large wooden table at a hospital in New York City. Four were doctors. One was a veterinarian, one was a secretary, and one was a community observer. Each had a thick stack of paper describing twenty to thirty plans for experiments using animals. Each plan explained the purpose of the experiment and how many animals would be needed. One question asked whether the animals would feel pain. If so, the researcher had to explain what kind of pain relief would be given.

For three hours, the people at the table considered the plans and asked even more questions. The first plan concerned surgery on dogs and a special patch to aid the healing of bone. "Where are we with this work?" asked one doctor. "Is this to train doctors to perform surgery with techniques we already know?"[1]

"I would rather these people get trained operating on the skull of a dog than on the skull of a two-year-old," answered another.[2]

"This is not training," explained a third physician. "They are using a new type of material to see how it works on the bones of the skull."[3]

After much discussion, the plan was put aside. The committee wanted to ask a plastic surgeon and a bone specialist to review the plan. Next the committee considered an experiment on rabbits and a specific area of the brain. The researcher wanted to study how rabbits react after a certain nerve is cut. "Are the lab workers trained to care for rabbits who have had this type of surgery?" asked a member of the committee. "Do they know anything about this type of brain damage already?"[4] For twenty minutes, the committee checked and rechecked the plan. Finally, they sent it back to the researcher. It would not be approved until the researcher supplied more

Animals Used in Research in the United States

Rats, Mice, & Birds	12,100,000*	Apes & Monkeys	56,381
Rabbits	309,322	Sheep	33,048
Guinea Pigs	272,797	Cats	26,091
Hamsters	217,079	Other Farm Animals	52,699
Dogs	75,429	Other Animals	150,987
Pigs	73,995		

*Because rats, mice, and birds are not covered under the Animal Welfare Act, their use is not reported to the government. This number is an estimate, based on the belief that rats, mice, and birds make up 90 percent of the animals in laboratories.

Source: U.S. Government: Animal and Plant Health Inspection Service, fiscal year 1997.

information. That's what happened to most of the plans. Only a few were approved that day or turned down completely.

The committee described above is the Animal Care and Use Committee (ACUC) of Columbia Presbyterian Medical Center, a major research institution. By law, all animal research funded by the federal government must be supervised by a committee like the one at Columbia. At Columbia, the Animal Care and Use Committee must approve all experiments done on live animals. Among ACUC members must be a veterinarian, a member of the general public, and a scientist who understands research methods.[5]

The Animal Welfare Act of 1966

The rules on Animal Care and Use committees are part of the Animal Welfare Act. The original Animal Welfare Act, called the Laboratory Animal Welfare Act of 1966, was designed to guard against the theft of household pets. It set standards for the handling, housing, feeding, and care of animals, including those in laboratories.[6] The law has been changed several times. In the current version, researchers are required to check whether a nonanimal experiment would provide the same information.[7] The law also allows unannounced inspections of laboratories. Painkillers must be given to animals that need them, except when the painkillers would interfere with research findings.[8] Also, attention must be given to the emotional well-being of animals. Dogs have to be exercised. Apes and monkeys must have toys. They must be housed in groups unless being with other animals would ruin the experiment.[9]

The Animal Welfare Act covers cats, dogs,

nonhuman primates (like apes and monkeys), hamsters, guinea pigs, rabbits, and other warm-blooded animals. Fish and birds are not included, nor are rats and mice, the most frequently used animals in research. However, Animal Care and Use Committees are supposed to check on all the animals in the laboratories in their institutions, even those not directly mentioned in the law. In 1990, the Animal Legal Defense Fund and the Humane Society sued to extend coverage of the Animal Welfare Act to mice, rats, and birds. The court ruled that animal welfare groups did not have the right to sue. The court said that the well-being of the people

*T*his cat, which had an electrode implanted in its head as part of a research experiment, was later rescued from Texas Tech University.

bringing the suit was not directly involved. The animal welfare groups argued that since animals themselves cannot sue, human beings must do so on their behalf. The court did not accept that argument, and the animal welfare groups lost the case. In 1998, the American Anti-Vivisection Society filed another petition with the United States Department of Agriculture. The petition asks that mice, rats, and birds be treated according to the rules of the Animal Welfare Act.[10]

Pound Seizure and Other State Laws

Every community in the United States has a pound—a place where stray or unwanted dogs and cats are taken. Some of these animals are reunited with their owners, and some are adopted as pets. Sadly, more than 10 million dogs and cats are not claimed. After a waiting period, they are put to death.

For every hundred animals killed in a pound, one is sold to a laboratory.[11] Thirteen states have pound seizure laws that forbid the release of pound animals for research. Five states require the release of pound animals to research labs, and the others permit pound seizure or let local communities decide.

Pound seizure laws are intended to protect family pets that might have gotten lost. Critics of pound seizure laws say that the waiting period gives owners enough time to find their lost pets. They point out that unclaimed animals are put to death anyway. Supporters of pound seizure laws believe that the extra protection is important. Many states have other laws to protect animals used in research.

Twenty states license research facilities and require certain standards of housing and cleanliness.

Protection for Researchers

The Animal Enterprise Protection Act of 1992 is a federal law that protects researchers and their laboratories from animal rights extremists. Twenty-three states have similar laws. Most of the laws call for severe penalties if information or laboratory equipment is destroyed or if animals are stolen. Like everyone else in the United States, animal rights groups have the right to free speech. However, threatening or dangerous behavior is specifically forbidden.[12]

Animal Welfare Laws in Other Countries

The first animal welfare law was passed in Great Britain in 1876. The Cruelty to Animals Act allowed experiments on animals, but it set up a licensing system for laboratories. The idea was that a lab would not receive a license unless it treated animals humanely. A little over a century later, the Animals Scientific Procedures Act of 1986 required British scientists to seek out in vitro methods. In 1992 the European Parliament, a governing body, passed a law setting a deadline for the marketing of cosmetics that are tested on animals. The law states that only nonanimal tested products can be sold in the European Economic Community countries after January 1, 1998. The deadline was then extended to 2000.[13]

Chapter 6

Dissection

I think you should be mature enough to understand the life you are taking," says Kelly, a high school senior.[1] Kelly is speaking of dissection. Recently Kelly, who wants to be a veterinarian, asked her school to run a special class on dissection. The class would not teach dissection techniques or anatomy (body structure) as ordinary classes do. Instead, the students would read essays explaining the arguments for and against dissection. Students would be encouraged to make a thoughtful choice—to dissect or to complete an alternate assignment.

Challenges to Dissection

Alternate assignments were not permitted in the 1920s when dissection became an important part of biology classes.[2] Dissection was considered the best way to teach young people about the anatomy of various animals, the differences between species, and evolution. For many years, the practice was seldom questioned. As the animal rights movement gained strength in the 1980s, supporters began to challenge dissection in science classes. "Put the 'life' back into biology" became a popular slogan.[3]

Some objections to dissection are grounded in morality. We do not have the right to take the life of an animal just to teach children about its nerves or digestive system, opponents say. Or as one Indiana student commented, "Animals are just as alive as we are. They have feelings. They have families."[4] Another student said, "I don't feel it's right to harm any animals just for a grade."[5]

Some teachers fear that dissection will teach students that animal life is unimportant. As Randall Lockwood of The Humane Society of the United States said, "Carving up a frog doesn't teach a student to think. . . . It teaches that living things . . . can be bought and thrown out at the end of class."[6] Critics of dissection believe that it may discourage students from going into science careers. As one animal rights group says, " . . . the best . . . scientists, who have a deep respect for animal life, may end up dropping out of a field they love because they refuse to take part in senseless killing."[7]

Other dissection critics are concerned about the environment. About 6 million animals a year are killed so that they can be dissected in American schools. Large companies raise some of these animals specifically for dissection. However, some are obtained from the wild. Removing animals from their natural environment may upset the balance of nature.

Arguments for Dissection

"There is no substitute for looking at a real animal. It is and always will be different from looking at a diagram or a model. It is the difference between something in a book and something in real life," says Juliet Bryant, a ninth-grade biology teacher.[8] "When you are looking at a picture or a diagram," adds Mary Elizabeth Wilson, also a high school science teacher, "you are looking at someone else's interpretation of the animal. Dissection teaches you that real life . . . does not always match the picture."[9] Steven Weinberg, founder of an organization called Educators for Responsible Science, says that many students have benefited from dissection lessons. Their interest in science was sparked. "They've gone on to become nurses, doctors, or other professionals" in the health fields.[10]

According to supporters, if a lesson is done correctly, students will take it seriously. They gain even more respect for the miracles of life, supporters say. "The best way to value something is to understand it," comments Juliet Bryant.[11]

Dissection and the Law

In 1987, a California high school student named Jenifer Graham refused to dissect a frog. She received a low grade in her biology course. Jenifer sued. The court said that Jenifer had to perform a dissection, but she could use a frog that had died of natural causes instead of one that had been killed especially for laboratory or school use. No such frog could be found. Jenifer was eventually given a good grade for the alternative work she had done in her biology course.[12]

Several states, including California, Florida, Maryland, New York, Pennsylvania, and Rhode Island, now have laws saying that students who object to dissection may complete another type of assignment instead. Jenifer helped found a dissection hot line, 1-800-922-FROG, for students needing help in "objecting to dissection." The hot line explains the law, provides a strategy for dealing with school officials, and suggests alternate assignments.[13]

Alternatives to Dissection

Instead of dissecting, students may use a computer program to analyze the body structures of animals. They may watch a film of a biology teacher dissecting an animal, or they may work with a plastic model. Other assignments focus on the natural behavior of living animals. Students go on nature trips to observe animals in the wild, or they visit zoos. In some cases they bring a living animal into the classroom and study its habits over.

Chapter 7

The Case for Animal Research

They need to know *why* I'm alive and why *they* are alive and benefiting from the responsible use of animals in medical research." That's the message Patty Wood wants to give to animal rights activists. Wood has received two transplanted kidneys. Once Wood told an animal rights protester, "I am alive because I've had a kidney transplant." Wood says that the man "yelled that I should be dead and that the rats and mice that saved my life should be alive."

After this experience, Wood began to investigate the issue of animals in research. She feels that it is her responsibility "as a person who loves animals and who is alive because of research, to make sure that the animals are treated right."[1]

Speciesism?

Dr. Ralph Dell, head of the Institute for Laboratory Animal Resources, says, "They call me a speciesist and I am. Like most humans I have a hierarchy [order of importance] of what I defend. I defend my family. I defend my work family. I defend human beings. I will use other animals in research that will defend or improve human life."[2]

Dell speaks from personal experience. Some years ago he began a series of experiments on puppies. He was trying to discover a feeding solution for babies who were born too early. The puppies died. However, Dell's solution now feeds infants all over the United States. Dell explains, "Survival of [the smallest] kids . . . has gone from something like 15 percent to something like 85 percent. I feel good about that. Do I feel good about having killed a bunch of puppies? That was very difficult."[3]

Benefits to Medicine

In 1870, about a quarter of all Americans died before the age of twenty-five and half died by age fifty. Now only 3 percent of Americans die before age twenty-five and only 10 percent die before age fifty. Only a few years ago, about 20 percent of cancer patients lived more than five years after their disease was discovered. Presently about 50 percent survive five years or longer.[4] In the 1950s, heart ailments were frequently fatal. Now more than four hundred thousand people a year have open-heart surgery in the United States.[5] Work with animals contributed to all these advances. In fact, about two thirds of the Nobel Prizes for Medicine or Physiology (the study of how the body functions) awarded since 1901 have been made for discoveries involving the use of animals.[6] Animal rights activists point out that although the prize-winning scientists used animals, they also worked in vitro. The activists believe that the discoveries made through in vitro methods were

Discoveries Made Through Animal Experimentation

Vaccines protecting against:

✓ Anthrax   ✓ Influenza
✓ Distemper   ✓ Parvovirus
✓ Feline Leukemia ✓ Pneumonitis
✓ Fowl Pox   ✓ Rabies
✓ Infectious Hepatitis ✓ Tetanus

Treatments for:

✓ Arthritis   ✓ Parasites
✓ Brucellosis   ✓ Some cancers
✓ Heartworm   ✓ Surgery for horses
✓ Infertility   ✓ Tuberculosis

Source: Incurably Ill For Animal Research

more important than those involving animal work. However, those who support animal research disagree.

Scientists who use animals in research note that humans share more than two hundred fifty diseases with animals of other species—diseases like diabetes and those affecting the heart and kidneys. When a treatment is developed, it may be used for both people and their pets.

Is In Vitro Research a Substitute?

Supporters of the use of animals in laboratories welcome techniques that reduce the need for animals. However, they say that nothing can replace animals completely. A science committee of the European Economic Community recently decided that current in vitro tests could not yet guarantee the safety of personal care products. The American Medical Association (AMA) states that in vitro research "cannot reproduce exactly the . . . biological system provided by live animals."[7]

Animal activists suggest that computer modeling programs and mathematical predictions take the place of some animal research. Again, the AMA disagrees because "much about the body and the various biological systems of humans and animals is not known,"[8] and a computer cannot be programmed with enough information to give an accurate result. The Congressional Office of Technology Assessment (OTA) reported that it is not possible to make a computer program that would substitute for a living animal. Dell, who used computers for biomedical research, says that computers "help design experiments, but they cannot replace making observations and having data (information) from actual experiments."[9]

Scientists who support animal research say that in vitro tests provide only limited information. They test only one specific thing. In animal experiments, a scientist checking for liver damage may find that the liver is not affected by the test drug, but the heart is. Such damage might not show up in an in vitro test. Biomedical researchers know that animals are not exactly the same as human beings. However, researchers note that animals and human beings share similar body chemicals, nervous systems, and reactions to infection or injury.

Unnecessary Research?

Animal rights supporters also charge that much unnecessary research is performed on animals. The AMA answers that research involving animals is very expensive. An example is the budget for a group of twenty dogs used in one experiment. Besides the scientist's salary, the budget included funds for an animal technician, a veterinarian, cages, food, and litter. The dogs' expenses came to almost fifty thousand dollars per year.[10] The AMA states that "because funding is limited in science, only high-quality research is able to compete effectively for support."[11] The National Institutes of Health, which funds most of the biomedical research in the United States, reviews all proposals for experiments involving animals. Only 25 percent of the experiments that it approves can be funded.

Because of the way science works, some duplication *must* take place. When a new discovery is announced, a paper explaining how the experiment was done is published in scientific journals. Other scientists repeat the experiment to see whether the outcome is the same. If the experiment cannot be repeated, the researcher must recheck. Dell explains, "It might be a mistake, a fluke. If you can't repeat, you start a discussion about the original experiment."[12]

Laboratory Conditions

If you take a walk through the research wing at Columbia Presbyterian Medical Center, you will see a large room that has ten to twelve cages in it, each containing a monkey. The metal cages are arranged in a semicircle. In some cages, babies cling to their mothers. The monkeys are pair-housed—two cages are connected on the side so that the monkeys can groom each other through the bars. Looking through the front of the cage, all the monkeys can see and hear every animal in the room.

Dr. Reginald Miller is the chief of veterinary medicine at the Columbia Institute of Comparative Medicine. Along with three other vets, he supervises the health and living conditions of all animals at the medical center. He takes care of tiny mice, as well as pigs and monkeys. Miller and his staff care about

*W*yoming police chief Tim World gives a citation to the PETA rabbit and other group members for distributing literature on private property without a permit.

the animals. When he enters a room, he calls out, "Hello there!" According to Miller, "They feel better when they hear me coming before they see me."[13]

In one room are shelves of plastic boxes with screened lids. Each box is about the size of a large shoe box and contains three or four mice. "We don't single house them," explains the veterinarian, "because they are social animals."[14] The mice have shredded material for bedding. If they are pregnant, they are given little cotton squares to make into a nest.

In another room larger plastic boxes hold rats, three or four to a container. In still another room are pigs and sheep, and in one area, dogs. These bigger animals are in metal pens about four feet by seven feet. Sheep are housed in flocks. One section of the research wing holds several operating rooms. Each contains the same type of equipment as operating rooms for human beings. In a recovery room, several animals sleep behind glass-walled, individual compartments.

In another room is a carbon dioxide chamber. When the experiments are over, many animals are unable to recover. Others must be dissected after death to provide the scientists with information necessary to the experiment. These animals are put to death in the chamber quickly and painlessly.

Of course, not all laboratories are exactly like the one at Columbia Presbyterian. However, most observers agree that because of new laws and the attention of animal activists, conditions for the animals have gotten better in recent years.[15]

What about the horrible pictures that animal rights activists display? According to a Department of Agriculture Report, 94 percent of all laboratory animals are in pain-free experiments or are given pain relievers during the experiment.[16]

Dell says, "Every once in a while you run into someone who doesn't care. In any human enterprise [activity] there are always a few who give the rest of us a bad name."[17] When bad conditions are found in a research environment, the work may be stopped. Only when the Animal Care and Use Committee is satisfied that the conditions have been corrected can work begin again.

Chapter 8

The Case Against Animal Research

When Jonathan Balcombe was in college, he saw some white rabbits lying on their backs. Little cups were attached to their bellies. Balcombe says, "They looked very stressed. I found out later that they were strapped down so that insects could bite them."[1] A scientist was studying the insects for another reason. He needed the rabbits only as a food source.

Balcombe majored in biology and now has a doctorate in animal behavior. But he was very upset by what he saw. Later, he became a member of People for the Ethical Treatment of Animals (PETA). Now he works for The Humane Society of the United States. Balcombe's personal view is that no one should ever perform experiments on an animal unless the work will help that particular animal.

Dr. Elliot Katz, founder and president of In Defense of Animals, agrees. "In the United States there were once people who argued in favor of slavery . . . but what seemed acceptable then is now looked back upon as something that is very unacceptable."[2] Katz believes that "we have a moral obligation to stop harming creatures simply because we are stronger and more powerful than they are."[2]

An Unnatural Life

According to Balcombe, the attention of the animal rights movement has improved physical conditions in laboratories. "There is little doubt that things are better for the average animal in research now than they were thirty or forty years ago," he says. However, he feels it is not enough to require veterinary care or cages of a certain size. He says, "We tend to think only about the actual experiment, but most of the time the animals are just sitting around in their cages . . . day in and day out, week in and week out, for months or years."[3]

Animal Protection Laws: Are They Strong Enough?

The Animal Welfare Act amendments are only a step in the right direction, in the view of animal activists. Rats, mice, birds, and fish are not covered. Katz also criticizes the law because it only deals with the housing, transportation, and sanitation" of animals. One section of the Animal Welfare Act says that the law is not allowed to interfere with the design, outline, or performance of actual research.[4] If a section of the law interferes with the experiment, the requirement is dropped.

Another problem is the pain that animals suffer during experiments. The Department of Agriculture reports that during 1997, about one hundred thousand animals were in distress and were given no painkillers during experiments. (No painkillers are given if the drugs would interfere with the results of the experiment.) Another 480,000 were in distress

*T*hese three beagles were among the forty that were scheduled for use in research experiments. Part of the research involved breaking the dogs' legs. Because of protest the beagles were not used.

but were given painkillers. Animal activists believe that these numbers are too low. The researchers themselves are responsible for reporting the number of animals in pain. According to one study, researchers underreported the number of painful experiments. The scientists were not deliberately lying. They just did not realize that the animals were suffering.[5]

Other critics of the Animal Welfare Act say that enforcement is a problem. Only seventy-one inspectors are in charge of more than thirteen thousand laboratories, as well as all the animal dealers, transporters, and exhibitors in the nation. Opponents of animal research believe that this number of inspectors cannot possibly guarantee conditions in so many places. In 1992, government officials selected twenty-six institutions at random to see whether they were fulfilling their responsibilities. Twelve were not.[6] Many laboratories belong to private certifying organizations. However, if a laboratory is not well run, it might not choose to be inspected privately.

Does Animal Research Save Lives?

Milrinone is a heart drug. In an experiment on heart disease, it was once given to rats whose hearts had been artificially stopped. Milrinone increased the survival rate of the rats. However, when Milrinone was given to humans with heart problems, their death rate increased by 30 percent.[7] In 1983, Pfizer, a major drug company, compared the information from animal experiments with that of human records to see what substances cause cancer. The animal tests were no better than flipping a coin at predicting cancer risk. A United States government report on drugs approved by the Food and Drug Administration between 1976 and 1985 found that over half of newly approved drugs caused more serious side effects than expected when put on the market. The drugs had to be withdrawn or given new warning labels.[8] Another study compared the irritation in rabbit eyes and human eyes caused by different household products. The eye irritation differed by a factor of 18 to 250.

Scientists who oppose the use of animals in research believe that we simply cannot compare the reactions of an animal with that of a human being. Dr. Kenneth Melmon, a drug researcher at the University of California, notes, "In most cases, the animal tests cannot predict what will happen when the drug is given to man."[9] Furthermore, because laboratory animals live in unnatural conditions, stress may affect the results of the experiments.

An Old Way of Thinking

According to some animal activists, biomedical research continues because scientists are used to working that way. Katz says, "The people in power who decide where the research dollars are going are from the 'old school' and don't know any other way to conduct research except with animals."[10]

The American Anti-Vivisection Society charges that "many scientists build their careers on animal experiments and forget that it is human disease which needs to be studied."[11]

In some countries traditional science education is changing. In the Netherlands, for example, researchers who plan to do research on animals must take a special class. Students learn how to design an experiment so that it causes the least discomfort to the animals involved. One assignment for the course is to find a way of answering the same question with an in vitro experiment.

A Misuse of Money

Opponents of animal research would like to see more training programs like the one in the

Companies That Do Not Test Their Products on Animals

Adrian Arpel	Clinique
Almay Hypo-Allergenic	Crabtree and Evelyn
America's Finest Products	Estee Lauder
Amway Corporation	John Paul Mitchell Systems
Andrew Jergens Company	Liz Claiborne Cosmetics
Aveda	Nexxus
Avon	Nordstrom Cosmetics
Bath and Body Works	Pathmark
Benetton Cosmetics	Redken Laboratories
Body Shop	Sally Hansen
Caswell-Massey	Tom's of Maine
Chanel	Victoria's Secret

Source: PETA and the American Anti-Vivisection Society

Note: This is not a complete list. For additional information, write to PETA or to the American Anti-Vivisection Society (see p. 56).

Netherlands. They also want more of the scarce research dollars to go to the prevention of disease. For example, in the last twenty years fewer Americans have died from heart disease than in previous decades. Some studies show that changes in diet and lifestyle are responsible for most of the improvement in the death rate from heart disease. Analyzing the ten leading causes of death in the United States, the Centers for Disease Control found that lifestyle and environmental factors cause 70 percent of early deaths.[12] Katz says,

> Just think what would happen if the $6 billion to $8 billion dollars spent each year on animal experiments were used to fund prevention and care instead. . . . What if the money had been spent to educate people, particularly children, about diet and tobacco and the proper use of alcohol? You would have a far healthier population.[13]

In Vitro Research

Dean Smith, an animal activist, states that "most [activists] believe that there are alternatives for *some* animal experiments, and that the scientific community should be actively striving [trying] to create more."[14] He adds that he knows of no activists who believe that the in vitro techniques now available can completely take the place of animal-based research. Nevertheless, Smith thinks that animal research is morally wrong and should be stopped anyway.

Many activists point out specific animal tests that they believe could have been done in vitro. Katz criticizes research involving brain surgery. "Now they have scanning techniques to study the human brain," he says. "You don't need to insert anything into an animal or a human to see how our own brains work."[15]

Some scientists believe that in vitro experiments can actually improve on animal-based research. Ron Alison, a doctor who studies cancer, states that "non-animal models are more sophisticated in many areas than the animal models."[16] Information from ten thousand cells allows the researcher to draw a more accurate conclusion than data from a small number of whole animal experiments.

Also, activists say that in vitro results come in much more quickly than work done on animals. Safety tests on chemicals done with animals take three to eight years to complete. In vitro tests on cells supply safety information in only a few days.

*T*wo members of PETA dressed as monkeys in prison suits to protest what they say is Proctor & Gamble's lethal poisoning of animals in testing their products.

Unnecessary Research

Balcombe also feels that much unnecessary work is done. "It has been known for a long time that babies need adult love and care in order to develop properly. But experiments in which infant animals are raised alone are still being performed," he comments.[17] The American Anti-Vivisection Society reports that more than seven thousand animals have taken part in this type of experiment in the last thirty years. Yet, the society concludes that only one experiment had a direct effect on the treatment of human beings. From 1993 to 1994, doctors at the State University of New York at Stonybrook studied AIDS. Using tissue samples taken from women with AIDS, they determined an important way that women become infected. After this work was done, researchers at New York University purposely infected female rhesus monkeys with SIV, a relative of the virus that causes AIDS in humans. Researchers found the same information that the university scientists had already published.[18]

Those who oppose experiments with animals would have liked to save the lives of the New York University monkeys. In fact, they would like to save the lives of all the animals in laboratories. Their mission can be summed up in this statement by artist Leonardo da Vinci: "The time will come when men such as I will look upon the murder of animals as they now look upon the murder of men."[19]

For Animal Experimentation

Animal and Plant Health Inspection Service
14th and Independence Avenue SW
Washington, DC 20250
(202) 447-3668
Web site:
www.aphis.usda.gov/ac

Association for Assessment and Accreditation of Laboratory Animal Care International (AAALAC)
11300 Rockville Pike, Suite 1211
Rockville,
Maryland 20852-3035
(301) 231-5353
Web site:
www.aaalac.org

Incurably Ill for Animal Research
9525 South Seventy-Ninth Avenue
Hickory Hills,
Illinois 60457
(708) 598-7787

NIMH Office of Animal Research Issues
5600 Fishers Lane
Room 17c-26
Rockville, Maryland 20857
(301) 443-1639

Against Animal Experimentation

The American Anti-Vivisection Society
801 Old York Road #204
Jenkintown,
Pennsylvania 19046-1685
1-800-SAY-AAVS
Web site: www.aava.org

Animal's Agenda
1301 S. Baylis Street
Suite 325
P.O. Box 25881
Baltimore, MD 21224
(410) 675-4566
Web Site:
www.animalsagenda.org

Animal Legal Defense Fund
127 Fourth Street
Petaluma,
California 94952-3005
(707) 769-7771

People for the Ethical Treatment of Animals (PETA)
P.O. Box 42516
Washington, DC 20015
(301) 770-PETA
Web site:
www.peta-online.org

Physicians Committee for Responsible Medicine
P.O. Box 6322
Washington, DC 20015
(202) 686-2210

Introduction

1. Author interview with Jonathan Balcombe, August 27, 1997.

2. Author interview with John Miller, August 27, 1997.

3. Madhusree Mukerjee, "Trends in Animal Research," *Scientific American*, February 1997, p. 86.

4. Department of Agriculture Animal and Plant Health Inspection Service Web site (www.aphis.usda.gov).

5. Ibid.

Chapter 1. A Historical View of Animals in Research

1. Genesis 1:28.

2. David Masci, "Fighting Over Animal Rights," *CQ Researcher*, August 2, 1996, p. 682.

3. John C. Petricciani and Ethel Thurston, "Regulation, Abolition, or Alternative Research," *American Fund for Alternatives to Animal Research*, undated pamphlet, p. 2.

4. William R. Hendee, Jerod M. Loeb, Steven J. Smith, and M. Roy Schwarz, "Human vs. Animal Rights," *Journal of the American Medical Association*, November 17, 1989, p. 2716.

5. James C. Whorton, "Animal Research," *Encyclopedia of Bioethics*, vol. 1, ed. Warren Thomas Reich (New York: Macmillan Library Reference, 1995), p. 145.

6. Ibid., p. 143.

7. J. J. McCoy, *Animals in Research*, (New York: Watts, 1993), p. 15.

8. William R. Hendee, Jerod M. Loeb, Steven J. Smith, and M. Roy Schwarz, "Use of Animals in Biomedical Research," *AMA White Paper*, 1989, p. 4.

9. Robert Temple, *The Genius of China* (New York: Simon & Schuster, 1986), p. 133.

10. *The History of Science and Technology*, vol. 1 (New York: Facts On File, 1988), p. 86.

11. Hendee et al., "Human vs. Animal Rights," p. 2716.

12. Jack H. Botting and Adrian R. Morrison, "Animal Research is Vital to Medicine," *Scientific American*, February, 1997, pp. 83–84.

13. David Petechuk, "Ivan Petrovich Pavlov," *Notable 20th Century Scientists*, vol. 3, ed. Emily J. McMurray (New York: Gale, 1995), p. 1550.

14. American Anti-Vivisection Society, "Problems with Product Testing," 1996, unpaged pamphlet.

15. "Cruelty-free": Does Anybody Really Know What It Means?" *iiFARsighted Report*, Winter 1996, p. 2.

Chapter 2. Animal Welfare and Animal Rights

1. William R. Hendee, Jerod M. Loeb, Steven J. Smith, and M. Roy Schwarz, "Human vs. Animal Rights," *Journal of the American Medical Association*, November 17, 1989, p. 2717.

2. James C. Whorton, "Animal Research," *Encyclopedia of Bioethics*, vol. 1, ed. Warren Thomas Reich (New York: Macmillan Library Reference, 1995), p. 145.

3. Joanne Zurlo, Deborah Rudacille, and Alan M. Goldberg, *Animals and Alternatives in Testing* (New York: Mary Ann Liebert, Inc. 1994), p. 37.

4. Julie Catalano, *Animal Welfare* (New York: Chelsea, 1994), pp. 23–25.

5. Whorton, p. 146.

6. Madhusree Mukerjee, "Trends in Animal Research," *Scientific American*, February 1997, p. 87.

7. Ibid.

8. Deborah Blum, *The Monkey Wars* (New York: Oxford, 1994), p. 122.

9. *PETA History: Compassion in Action*. PETA unpaged, undated pamphlet.

10. Blum, pp. 107, 113, 122.

11. Ibid., pp. 115–116.

Chapter 3. How Animals Are Used in Research and Testing

1. Marguerite Holloway, "Profile of Rita Levi-Montalcini: Finding the Good in the Bad," *Scientific American*, January 1993, pp. 32–33.

2. Deborah Blum, *The Monkey Wars* (New York: Oxford, 1994), p. 164.

3. Committee on the Use of Animals in Research, *Science, Medicine, and Animals* (Washington, D.C.: National Academy Press, 1991), p. 1.

4. Clarice Swisher, *Genetic Engineering* (San Diego: Lucent Overview Series, 1996), p. 31.

5. William R. Hendee, Jerod M. Loeb, Steven J. Smith, and M. Roy Schwarz, "Use of Animals in Biomedical Research," *AMA White Paper*, 1989, p. 5.

6. Swisher, pp. 46, 66–67.

7. Joanne Zurlo, Deborah Rudacille, and Alan M. Goldberg, *Animals and Alternatives in Testing* (New York: Mary Ann Liebert, 1994), pp. 12, 23–24.

8. Ibid., p. 10.

9. American Anti-Vivisection Society, *Problems with Product Testing*, December 1996, unpaged pamphlet.

10. The Johns Hopkins Center for Alternatives to Animal Testing, pamphlet, unpaged and undated.

Chapter 4. Testing Without Animals

1. Joanne Zurlo, Deborah Rudacille, and Alan M. Goldberg, *Animals and Alternatives in Testing* (New York: Mary Ann Liebert, 1994), p. 28.

2. American Anti-Vivisection Society, "Liberating the Laboratory," *Let's Liberate Science*, undated, p. 10.

3. Robert Sharpe, Human Tissue, *American Anti-Vivisection Society pamphlet*, pp. 2–3, 9.

4. *Animals, The Vital Link to Health and Safety*, National Institutes of Health pamphlet, 1992, p. 4.

5. "Alternatives in Product Testing," *Alternatives, AV Magazine*, December 1997, p. 12.

6. The Johns Hopkins School of Public Health Center for Alternatives to Animal Testing, *Adventures in Tier-Testing*, vol. 4, p. 6.

7. American Anti-Vivisection Society, "The Human Factor," *Let's Liberate Science*, undated, p. 7.

8. D.P. Southall and M.P. Samuels, *British Medical Journal*, February 1, 1992, pp. 265–266, quoted in American Anti-Vivisection Society, "The Human Factor," *Let's Liberate Science*, undated, p. 8.

9. Steve Stecklow, "New Food-Quality Act Has Pesticide Makers Doing Human Testing," *Wall Street Journal*, September 28, 1998.

10. American Anti-Vivisection Society, "Progress Without Pain," *Let's Liberate Science*, undated, p. 1.

11. Madhusree Mukerjee, "Trends in Animal Research," *Scientific American*, February 1997, p. 89.

12. Zurlo, p. 25.

13. The Johns Hopkins School of Public Health Center for Alternatives to Animal Testing, p. 6.

Chapter 5. Animal Experimentation and the Law

1. Meeting witnessed by author, October 2, 1997.

2. Ibid.

3. Ibid.

4. Ibid.

5. Public Law 99-198 99 Stat 1645.

6. Public Law No. 89-544.

7. 7 U.S.C. 2143(a)(3)(B)

8. Public Law 91-579 84 Stat 1560.

9. Public Law 99-198 99 Stat. 1645.

10. Petition of the AAVS.

11. Foundation for Biomedical Research, *The Use of Pound Animals in Biomedical Research and Education* (Washington, D.C.: Foundation for Biomedical Research, 1990).

12. Public Law 102-346 106 Stat. 928.

13. Johns Hopkins Center for Alternatives in Testing Web site.

Chapter 6. Dissection

1. Author interview, October 8, 1997. Student's name withheld upon request.

2. Kathryn Winiarski, "Blackboard: Dissection Hot Line Cuts It," *The New York Times*, January 6, 1991, sec. 4A, p. 10.

3. *Putting the Life Back into Biology*, Humane Society of the United States, pamphlet, undated, p. 1.

4. Dirk Johnson, "Frogs' Best Friends, Students Who Won't Dissect Them," *The New York Times*, May 29, 1997, p. 16.

5. Winiarski, p. 10.

6. Madeline Chinnici, "A Frog's Day in Court," *Discover*, December 1987, p. 43.

7. *Objecting to Dissection*, Animal Legal Defense Fund Pamphlet, 1997, p. 3.

8. Author interview with Juliet Bryant, March 13, 1998.

9. Author interview with Mary Beth Wilson, March 13, 1998.

10. Peggy McCarthy, "School Officials Debate the Value of Dissection," *The New York Times*, August 18, 1991, sec. 12CN, p. 6.

11. Author interview with Juliet Bryant.

12. Lisa Ann Hepner, *Animals in Education* (Albuquerque, N.M.: Richmond), p. 69.

13. Johnson, p. 16.

Chapter 7. The Case for Animal Research

1. Author interview with Patty Wood, August 27, 1997.

2. Author interview with Ralph Dell, October 2, 1997.

3. Ibid.

4. *Issues and Answers*, pamphlet published by the Illinois Society for Medical Research and the Incurably Ill for Animal Research, undated, p. 1.

5. Jack H. Botting and Adrian R. Morrison, "Animal Research is Vital to Medicine," *Scientific American*, February 1997, p. 84.

6. William R. Hendee, Jerod M. Loeb, Steven J. Smith, and M. Roy Schwarz, "Use of Animals in Biomedical Research," *AMA White Paper*, 1989, p. 1.

7. Hendee et al., p. 18.

8. Ibid.

9. Author interview with Ralph Dell.

10. Committee on Preservation of Laboratory Animal Resources, "Important Laboratory Animal Resources," *ILAR News*, vol. 32, no. 4, 1990, p. A31.

11. *Science, Medicine*, and Animals, p. 9.

12. Author interview with Ralph Dell.

13. Author interview with Reginald Miller, October 2, 1997.

14. Ibid.

15. Hendee et al., p. 2.

16. Committee on the Use of Animals in Research, *Science, Medicine and Animals* (Washington, D.C.: National Academy Press, 1991), p. 23.

17. Author interview with Ralph Dell.

Chapter 8. The Case Against Animal Research

1. Author interview with Jonathan Balcombe, August 27, 1997.

2. Author interview with Elliot Katz, August 5, 1997.

3. Author interview with Jonathan Balcombe.

4. U.S.C. 2131-2159; 7 CFR 2.22, 2.80, and 371.2(g).

5. Mary T. Phillips, "Savages, Drunks, and Lab Animals: The Researcher's Perception of Pain," *Society and Animals*, vol. 1, no.1, pp. 61–81.

6. Madhusree Mukerjee, "Trends in Animal Research," *Scientific American*, February 1997, p. 92.

7. Medical Research Modernization Committee, *A Critical Look at Animal Experimentation* (New York: Medical Research Modernization Committee, 1998), p. 9.

8. *F.D.A. Drug Review: Postapproval Risks 1976–1985* (Washington, D.C.: U.S. General Accounting Office, April 1990).

9. K. L. Melmon, *Clinical Pharmacology and Therapeutics*, 1976, vol. 20, pp. 125–129, quoted in "What Is an Alternative?," *Liberate Science*, an American Anti-Vivisection Society publication, p. 4.

10. Author interview with Elliot Katz.

11. "Questions and Answers," *Health and Humane Research*, a publication of the American Anti-Vivisection Society.

12. "The Power of Prevention," *Health and Humane Research*, a publication of the American Anti-Vivisection Society.

13. Author interview with Elliot Katz.

14. Dean Smith, "A Critique of the AMA's White Paper," p. 11.

15. Author interview with Elliot Katz.

16. David Masci, "Fighting Over Animal Rights," *CQ Researcher*, August 2, 1996, p. 679.

17. Author interview with Jonathan Balcombe.

18. Neal D. Barnard and Stephen R. Kaufman, "Animal Research Is Wasteful and Misleading," *Scientific American*, February 1997, p. 82.

19. PETA Guide to Animal Liberation (Washington, D.C.: PETA, undated), unpaged.

Ames test—A test in which bacteria are exposed to chemicals. If the bacteria's genes show damage, the chemical is suspected of causing cancer in humans.

anesthetic—A drug that causes sleep or numbs pain.

antivivisection—A term referring to those who object to experiments on living animals.

biomedical research—Medical research on live animals.

culture—A procedure in which cells are grown in the laboratory.

dissection—Cutting into the dead body of an animal in order to study the body structures.

Draize tests—Tests on animals to see if chemicals irritate or damage the skin and eyes.

epidemiology—A scientific technique in which information on medical history, eating, exercise, and other habits is collected through surveys of large groups of people or from medical records.

HIV—The virus that causes the disease of AIDS in humans.

in vitro—Experiments done without living animals.

in vivo—Experiments performed on living animals.

LD50—A test in which a chemical is given to a group of living animals until half of the animals die.

Nerve Growth Factor—A body chemical that causes extra nerves to grow in tumors.

pound seizure laws—Laws that permit or require animals from pounds to be given to biomedical researchers.

SIV—The virus that causes the disease of AIDS in apes and monkeys.

speciesism—The belief that one species (that is, human beings) has more rights than other species.

tier testing—A technique where in vitro experiments rule out many chemicals before animal tests are tried.

tumor—A growth of cells that is not normal.

utilitarianism—A philosophy that says the welfare of human beings must be weighed against the bad effects an experiment has on animals.

vaccine—A medicine that prevents a specific disease.

vivisection—A term for research performed on live animals.

Glossary

The Animal Rights Handbook. Los Angeles: Living Planet Press, 1990.

Catalano, Julie. *Animal Welfare*. New York: Chelsea, 1994.

Cohen, Daniel. *Animal Rights*. Brookfield, Conn.: Millbrook Press, 1993.

Levine, Herb. *Animal Rights*. Austin, Tex.: Raintree Steck-Vaughn Publishers, Inc.

McCoy, J.J. *Animals in Research*. New York: Watts, 1993.

Newkirk, Ingrid. *Save the Animals!* Washington, DC: PETA, undated.

Sherry, Clifford J. *Animal Rights: A Reference Handbook*. Santa Barbara, Calif.: ABC-CLIO, Inc., 1994.

Swisher, Clarice. *Genetic Engineering*. San Diego: Lucent Overview Series, 1996.

Further Reading